Asnowy landscape. A beaming lamppost. A world where it is always winter and never Christmas. The opening scenes of C. S. Lewis's *The Lion, the Witch, and the Wardrobe* set the stage, and readers young and old await Aslan's return to Narnia, bringing with him the joy of Christmas.

While Lewis doesn't mention the birth of Christ specifically, he writes out of a deep sense of wonder and joy at the Incarnation as a world-transforming event: the Word becoming flesh (John 1:18). In one famous essay Lewis called it "The Grand Miracle."

You may be entering this Advent season with a sense of inadequacy. Perhaps your life is filled with great difficulty, the deep grief of loss, discouragement, financial concerns, addiction, depression, or even a sense that God is far from you.

The good news is that you are actually in a wonderful place to begin a meaningful Advent journey. For this season isn't about what we must accomplish, but rather about what God has already done in the miracle of the Incarnation. In fact all we need to do is invite God into the authentic reality of our messy, broken, complicated lives—to be transparently present to him in the midst of our weakness. How do we best do this? Slow down and spend time in quiet—as Jesus taught us—to read the words of Scripture and to listen to our God right where we are.

Christian History Institute and the Marion E. Wade Center have accordingly gathered together daily devotional reflections from scholars and Christian leaders who have been inspired by the writings of the seven authors collected by Wade and featured in *Christian History* issue #113, *The Seven Sages.* We've included a bonus offering based on a writing of Joy Davidman, Lewis's American wife. These authors are very different—ranging over several generations, with various occupations, and writing in a variety of genres. Some were members of the informal conversational group called the Inklings that gathered around Lewis and Tolkien; others were not. All, though, were united by two characteristics Lewis once used to describe the Inklings: "a tendency to write, and Christianity." And the Christianity that united them was grounded in a robust doctrine of God become Man.

Since Advent begins on a different day every year, we have chosen to begin with November 28—allowing for a full four weeks of Advent reflections. You may start on that day or on whatever day Advent begins in this year's liturgical calendar.

You will find reflections by scholars and novelists, administrators and pastors, actors and essayists, parents and children. Like the Wade authors who inspired them, they are united in being bowled over by the Grand Miracle of the Incarnation. We pray as you ponder these meditations this Advent that you will be brought anew to marvel at the birth of the Holy Child who came to redeem us by becoming one of us, and to say with joyful anticipation: "Come, Lord Jesus, come!"

Jennifer Woodruff Tait, *Christian History*
Marjorie Lamp Mead, Marion E. Wade Center

So [the shepherds] went with haste and found Mary
and Joseph, and the child lying in the manger.

(Luke 2:16, NRSV)

Lanterns in the snow

> *We must lay before Him what is in us,*
> *not what ought to be in us.*
>
> —C. S. Lewis, *Letters to Malcolm: Chiefly on Prayer*

The nativity is an extraordinary story, with angel choruses on one side and wise men bearing gold and frankincense and myrrh on the other. And into this grand and supernatural scene, God calls forth a group of shepherds, men with calloused hands, men who smell of livestock and open fields. In the midst of so much majesty, what do such ordinary, everyday people as shepherds have to offer?

Perhaps they brought along a lamb, a blanket, a lantern for the stable, or some food for the weary travelers. We are not told. But we do know this: the shepherds hastened to be present. They hurried to respond to what they had been given. They opened their hearts. They stood dumbfounded, witness to the miracle. Then they lingered.

As I prepare for Christmas, as I purchase gifts for family and friends, I wonder how I might follow their example. Tuning my heart to hear angel voices. Allowing my routines to be interrupted by the divine. Gaining wisdom to lay aside all else to behold the face of God. And finding the courage to come to Jesus just as I am.

In *Letters to Malcolm: Chiefly on Prayer*, C. S. Lewis reminds us of the appropriateness of the shepherds' gifts. Whatever else they may have brought to the stable, they laid aside their plans and chose to present themselves to Emmanuel, God-with-us.

In this busy Advent season, what does the Lord require of me? To be alert to the ways that the supernatural breaks through into my very ordinary life, to respond quickly to what I see and hear, to be no more and no less than who I truly am. And to discover—to my utter astonishment—that that is exactly the gift that my Lord God, King of the universe, has been waiting for.

Lord, prepare my heart this Advent. Amen.

Diana Pavlac Glyer teaches in the Honors College at Azusa Pacific University. She is the author of two books about Lewis, Tolkien, and the Inklings and has written a devotional called *Clay in the Potter's Hands*.

He was praying in a certain place, and after he had finished, one of his disciples said to him, "Lord, teach us to pray, as John taught his disciples."

(Luke 11:1, NRSV)

A meditative moment

And why should the good of anyone depend on the prayer of another? I can only answer with the return question, "Why should my prayer be powerless to help another?"

—George MacDonald, *Unspoken Sermons*, "Man's Difficulty Concerning Prayer"

Advent is a time for self-examination, a time for repentance, and a time to prepare ourselves spiritually. Therefore it is a time for prayer. *Lord, help me to overcome my sins. Lord, forgive me. Lord, how can I prepare to meet you?* All these petitions point to the future, to looking forward in expectation.

One Advent hymn captures some of those ideas: "Come Thou long-expected Jesus, born to set thy people free." We can identify with the Hebrew people waiting for their Messiah crying, "When will we be set free from our struggles?" And we also identify with the Christians represented in Revelation 6:10 crying, "How long, Lord?"

The Hebrews didn't understand the sort of Messiah that God would provide. When he came most didn't recognize him. Even though as Christians we know how God answered their prayers for a Messiah King, we are often in the dark as to our own future. Thus, when we pray, it is best not to have too many expectations of exactly how our prayers will be answered.

MacDonald looks at the mystery of prayer from the only perspective that makes sense—which is love. We don't know how God will work. Nor do we know how our own prayers can make any difference. But, like the Hebrew people of old, we know from experience that God is faithful and wants the best for us and for our loved ones.

Our Lord taught us to pray, "Thy kingdom come, Thy will be done." The kingdom of God is built on the expectation of faithful love. Our loving prayers are somehow a participation in that kingdom. And, as MacDonald says, "Why should my prayer be powerless to help another?"

Lord, you love me beyond my power of imagining.
From all that prevents me from loving you more, deliver me.
Help me to become a living prayer
for the good of those you have placed in my life. Amen.

Robert Trexler is an independent scholar with a particular interest in the works of George MacDonald. He is the president of Winged Lion Press, publisher of over 50 books specializing in Inklings-related topics, and the editor of *CSL: The Bulletin of the New York C. S. Lewis Society.*

Whoever claims to love God yet hates a brother or sister is a liar. For whoever does not love their brother and sister, whom they have seen, cannot love God, whom they have not seen.
(1 John 4:20, NIV)

Oxford street market

All men matter. You matter. I matter.
It's the hardest thing in theology to believe.

—G. K. Chesterton, "The Quick One," *The Scandal of Father Brown*

O ne of the good things about reading detective fiction, like Chesterton's Father Brown stories or the novels of Dorothy L. Sayers, is that it reminds us of the truth that all of us matter. Even if the murder victim was obnoxious, or completely insignificant in the eyes of the world, enormous quantities of time, money, and effort will be spent in bringing his or her killer to justice because murder is never justifiable. In detective fiction, as in the eyes of God, every life is important. At Christmas we celebrate our God, who became a human being and lived a human life so that all people might know him and find salvation.

Although it is sometimes hard for us to realize how much God loves us and our families and friends, it is often even harder to grasp his equally great love for some other people. How can such a bullying boss or corrupt politician matter to God? Or my friend's violent ex-husband? Or those drug addicts, immigrants, hoboes, gangsters...? We all have our own blind spots—those people we don't see through God's loving, compassionate eyes, but only through the lens of our own prejudices—and perhaps those whom we don't see at all, those we somehow don't even notice are there.

Yet the Bible tells us clearly that all people matter so much that if we can't love the ones we have seen, we can't really love God. It's as simple as that. For all people are made in God's image, and, if we look hard enough, we can see him in each and every one of them.

Dear God, thank you for your great love for us all.
Help me to realize how much all people matter and
to understand your love for those I find difficult. Amen.

Suzanne Bray is professor of English at Lille Catholic University in the north of France. She is also a lay reader in the Church of England. She is editor of *The Christ of the Creeds* by Dorothy L. Sayers.

The angel went to her and said, "Greetings,
you who are highly favored! The Lord is with you."
(Luke 1:28, NIV)

Snowy path

> *If we should ever grow brave,*
> *what on earth would become of us?*
>
> —Joy Davidman Lewis, "On Fear"

"Do not fear." It is one of the first things the angel Gabriel says to Mary as she is told that she will carry the Son of God. These three words are repeated over and over in the Bible, and yet how many times do we make decisions based on fear? How often do we plunge into those deep and dark waters? One might argue that Mary didn't truly have a choice (how could a devout young Jewish woman say "no" to a request from the living God?), but she did have the choice whether to surrender in faith or to grow in fear. And she chose trusting surrender, as did her husband, Joseph. They chose to believe the angel, to trust God, to become part of a larger redemptive story of humanity through the Divine.

This is, to say the least, an unexpected turn of events. Gabriel says, "Mary, you have found favor with God." We might, in her position, respond, "Favor? I found favor? I am pregnant out of wedlock, and I have to explain this to my betrothed and my family?" But instead Mary quickly responds, "May it happen to me according to your word."

How difficult that last line is when we dwell in fear instead of surrender. When the unexpected enters our lives, when our tight grip of control is torn from us, what remains? Do we enter into fear or into trust? This question is built into the quote from Joy Davidman, C. S. Lewis's wife, as she wrestled with her new-found faith: "If we should ever grow brave, what on earth would become of us?" She asked, "If Jesus told us, 'Do not fear' why don't we believe him?" Mary believed the angel. Do we believe the Son of God?

During this season of Advent, let us remember that when the unexpected arrives in our lives, possibly shattering all we have built or held dear, we, like Mary, must ask ourselves, "Do we fear or do we trust?" This is not a question that can be answered with simple platitudes; it is answered in the way in which we live our lives with Christ.

> *Dear Jesus, when the unexpected enters my life, please come alongside*
> *and help me to trust instead of fear, to surrender in spite of my tendency*
> *to cling, and to love you with the courage of Mary. Amen.*

Patti Callahan Henry is the *New York Times* best-selling author of 15 novels, including *Becoming Mrs. Lewis: The Improbable Love Story of Joy Davidman and C. S. Lewis*.

*Then Mary said, Here am I, the servant of the Lord.
Let it be with me according to your word. Then the
angel departed from her.*

(Luke 1:38 NRSV)

The Annunciation

[Mary]: When the Angel's message came to me, the Lord put a song into my heart. I suddenly saw that wealth and cleverness were nothing to God—no one is too unimportant to be His friend.

—Dorothy L. Sayers, *The Man Born to Be King*

Was Mary caught utterly unaware by the sudden angelic visitation? For generations all young Jewish women had held in their hearts the secret desire to be the mother of the One promised in Isaiah's prophecy. But for most that was only a dream, a tradition, an ambition unlikely to be fulfilled.

So why was Mary chosen for this relationship with the Most High God? In the moment reality surpassed the vision and was more than wishful thinking. Here's my reflection on the moment of Mary's astonishment:

> Mary, virgin, had no sittings, no chance to
> pose her piety, no novitiate for body
> or for heart. The moment was on
> her, unaware:
> the Angel in her room, the impossible
> demand...

As Sayers emphasized, Mary was young and inexperienced, a female in a male-dominated society. She lived in Nazareth, not the holy city of Jerusalem. She was pregnant and unmarried, open to rumor and conjecture, and probably illiterate. And the Angel had left her! She was alone, wondering what on earth to tell her mother, what on earth was being asked of her.

It's amazing that her heart was wide open to the impossible possibility that the Mighty One of Israel had chosen her! And the reality, overwhelming as it must have been, brought Mary a fresh purpose for her life: a village girl unprepared for a role that demanded of her—simply everything. No matter our own sense of inadequacy, of unpreparedness, such openness is at the heart of any act of faith.

> Still, the secret at her heart burns like a
> sun rising. How to hold it in—
> that which cannot be contained.
>
> She nestles into herself, half convinced it
> was some kind of good dream,
> she its visionary.
>
> But then, part dazzled, part prescient—
> she hugs her body, a pod with a seed
> that will split her.

Will we be like Mary, when God asks more of us than we think is possible? We remember Paul's challenge to each of us in our human, flawed condition: "Christ in you, the hope of glory." May we, too, become pregnant with God.

Loving God, in the immense scope of the universe, I am one small, very ordinary human being, but I long to show you my love. I offer you the best gift I have, my obedient heart. Amen.

Luci Shaw is writer in residence at Regent College and cofounder of Harold Shaw Publishers. Author of 11 volumes of poetry, she has also written Christian books on imagination, beauty, and daring. *The Generosity* is coming from Paraclete Press in 2020.

His mercy is for those
who fear him from
generation to generation.
(Luke 1:50 NRSV)

The Visitation

One must keep on pointing out that Christianity is a statement which, if false, is of no importance, and if true, of infinite importance. The one thing it cannot be is moderately important.

— C. S. Lewis, "Christian Apologetics"

*I*n faith, Mary, after accepting her call through the angel Gabriel to give birth to the Son of God, made haste on a three-day journey from her home in Nazareth to the hill country of Judah to visit her relative Elizabeth. Upon her arrival Elizabeth immediately confirmed that Mary was blessed for actively believing and acting on God's word. Mary had been chosen to play a vital role in the fulfillment of God's merciful rescue plan for the world through the Incarnation as God took on human form.

In response to this revelation, Mary was overcome and spontaneously sang a song of praise (now known as the Magnificat) in which she joyfully proclaimed that "God's mercy is for those who fear him from generation to generation."

The birth of Jesus Christ through Mary, an obedient, God-fearing woman, made possible God's great act of mercy in which he so loved the world that he gave his only Son, that whoever believes in him shall not perish but have everlasting life. Mary's song communicates the profound truth of Christianity that God's lifesaving mercy is available to those who fear God. Inherent in this truth also is the idea that those who do not fear God will not receive his mercy.

For this reason C. S. Lewis wrote, "One must keep on pointing out that Christianity is a statement which, if false, is of no importance, and if true, of infinite importance. The one thing it cannot be is moderately important."

Heavenly Father, as we reflect upon the miraculous birth of Jesus, the moment in which the Incarnation became a reality, let us thank God for Mary, who believed God and acted upon his word as being something of infinite importance. In the same way, let us not forget to thank you, God, for your mercy, poured out upon us through the atoning life and work of Jesus Christ on the cross. May we live every moment with the understanding that our Christian faith is of infinite importance as we prioritize our thoughts, words, and deeds. In the name of Jesus Christ, Amen.

Joel S. Woodruff is president of the C. S. Lewis Institute, Washington, D.C.

*For God's foolishness is wiser than human wisdom, and
God's weakness is stronger than human strength.*

(1 Corinthians 1:25, NRSV)

*Tolkien's writing desk, dip pen, and signature
in a first edition of* The Hobbit

The incarnation of God is an infinitely greater thing than anything I would dare to write.

—J. R. R. Tolkien, *The Letters of J. R. R. Tolkien*, Letter #181

I once met a theologian who was critical of what he saw as J. R. R. Tolkien's lack of expression of his faith, as there are no places of worship in Middle-earth. However the world of Middle-earth in its pre-Christian age is full of the presence of its divine maker, heralding the Incarnation of God himself in a future age.

Tolkien saw the creativity of storytellers as "sub-creation"—the world of the story is made in the image of the primary creation of God. In fact the storyteller himself or herself is made in the image of God; that image is distorted, but nevertheless still human. In his creation of the mythological and detailed world of Middle-earth—with its languages, peoples, and history—Tolkien extensively explores the increasing presence of God in many acts of providence and prophecy.

Angelic beings such as messengers, guardians, and helpers appear as incarnate human beings—think of Gandalf the wizard. Their appearance, as well as instances when elves marry mortals (such as Aragorn's marriage to Arwen), are just some of many foreshadowings and heraldings of the long-expected king—who, when he eventually comes, is in turn a foreshadowing of Christ the king's infinitely greater Incarnation in that future age. The apparent foolishness of the quest of hobbits Frodo and Sam to destroy the evil ring of power in the hell of Mordor foreshadows the apparent foolishness of death on the cross.

In their captivating way, Tolkien's stories are a deep reminder of the Incarnation of Jesus, the Son of God, as the glorious fulfillment of the increasing presence of God—the maker of heaven and earth. He came to the world we live in and experience as God-with-us, Emmanuel. Tolkien's fantasy history points us to real history in a vibrantly fresh way. Can you see your own creative self as an expression of the creator living through you?

Thank you, Lord Jesus, for entering the physical world of your own creation to be with us forever. May our creativity be a tangible reminder and reflection of your love. Amen.

Colin Duriez is the author of a number of books about Tolkien, Lewis, and the Inklings and received the Clyde S. Kilby Research Grant from the Marion E. Wade Center, Wheaton College, in 1994 for his work on the Inklings.

And the Word became flesh and lived among us, and we have seen his glory, the glory as of a father's only son, full of grace and truth.
(John 1:14, NRSV)

Christ the Saviour (Pantokrator)

The central miracle asserted by Christians is the Incarnation. They say that God became Man. Every other miracle prepares for this, or exhibits this, or results from this.

—C. S. Lewis, *Miracles*

The discovery of the Incarnation was transformative for Lewis. His initial conversion "was only to theism, pure and simple. Not Christianity. I knew nothing of the Incarnation," he wrote. "The god to whom I surrendered was not human. My training was like that of the Jews."

Thus Lewis's first step was to "give in" to the moral lawgiver of the Old Testament. However it quickly became apparent to him that to adequately appease this lawgiver who is absolute goodness is an impossible task. For as a sinful, finite being, Lewis realized that he was incapable of consistently doing what was right. His failure to keep the law left him with a deep sense of hopelessness. And as Lewis wrote to Sister Penelope, "This Lawgiver imparts despair rather than comfort (unless you add the Christian doctrine of the Atonement)."

But fortunately over time, Lewis came to realize that "Christianity tells us how God is the power behind the Moral Law and yet also a Person who forgives." The key here is understanding that God, the lawgiver, provides the necessary forgiveness to cover our failures.

And this is why we celebrate Advent. For, as Lewis explains, it is through Christ that "the demands of this law have been met on our behalf . . . [when] God Himself becomes a man to save man from God's disapproval." In other words, as the creeds explain, our very hopelessness is overcome by the Incarnation and atoning work of Christ who "for our salvation . . . came down from heaven . . . and was made man." To quote Lewis once again, our God "goes down to come up again and bring the whole ruined world up with Him."

God who became man. Truly the Grand Miracle.

Lord, may we see with open eyes, understanding minds, and enthralled hearts the true majesty of the Grand Miracle of your Incarnation. Come and transform us. Amen.

Max McLean is founder and artistic director of Fellowship for Performing Arts, a New York–based theater company creating theater from a Christian worldview to engage a diverse audience and whose productions include portrayals of Lewis's work onstage. He is also the voice of the NIV and KJV on Bible Gateway and the YouVersion Bible app.

In those days a decree went out from Emperor Augustus that all the world should be registered. This was the first registration and was taken while Quirinius was governor of Syria.
(Luke 2:34–35, NRSV)

Caesar Augustus

For Jesus Christ is unique—unique among gods and men.
There have been incarnate gods a-plenty,
and slain-and-resurrected gods not a few;
but He is the only God who has a date in history.

—Dorothy L. Sayers, *The Man Born to Be King*

Good old Quirinius! We encounter his name every time we read the story of the first Christmas. In accordance with the decree of Caesar Augustus, Mary and Joseph traveled to Bethlehem to register with the Romans. In his Gospel Luke confidently asserts that this was the first census "taken while Quirinius was governor of Syria" (Luke 2:2).

For a time some scholars doubted whether Luke knew quite what he was talking about. There was no "governor" of "Syria," they claimed. Yet later research confirmed that the Evangelist was using precisely the right term for exactly the right person. Quirinius really lived, and he was the governor of Syria after all!

Hearing Quirinius's distinctive name firmly roots the Incarnation in human history. Quirinius and Augustus were real people. Mary and Joseph were real people too—a humble Jewish carpenter and his faith-filled betrothed.

The baby who was born to them in Bethlehem was every bit as real. The Son of God came into the same everyday world that we live in—the world of imperial powers, government regulations, and long family trips back home. Jesus became one of us to save us. He is our Savior in flesh and blood.

Near the end of his Gospel, Luke introduces us to another Roman official: Pontius Pilate, who unjustly sentenced Jesus to death. If Quirinius helps us date the birth of Jesus, then Pilate confirms the time of his death.

Augustus, Pilate, and Quirinius remind us what is truly unique about Jesus Christ in the history of the world: his miraculous birth, atoning death, and bodily Resurrection really happened!

This is really good news for any real person who needs forgiveness and hopes one day to rise from the dead. Our salvation is as genuine as good old Quirinius.

Heavenly Father, thank you for sending your Son
to be my Savior in time and space. And thank you for
strengthening my faith by including facts of history
in the story of the gospel. In Jesus's name, Amen.

Philip Ryken is the president of Wheaton College and serves as a teaching elder in the Presbyterian Church in America.

*I thank my God every time I remember you,
constantly praying with joy in every one of my prayers
for all of you, because of your sharing in the gospel
from the first day until now.*

(Philippians 1:3–5 NRSV)

Mother and child share Christmas joy.

It is the heart that is not yet sure of its God
that is afraid to laugh in His presence.

—George MacDonald, *Sir Gibbie*

In college I had a friend who often laughed during prayer. Those of us who were more accustomed to solemnity were shocked at first, but soon we couldn't help smiling at the childlike, un-self-conscious delight that bubbled out of her when she was praising God. Her spontaneous giggle in the presence of the Holy felt holy to us.

George MacDonald would have loved her for it. What is more beautiful, he prompts us to consider again and again, than the pure joy of a childlike heart embraced by the most loving Father? The mute, abandoned boy in his novel *Sir Gibbie* is so delighted upon hearing the story of the prodigal son that he bursts into "a wild laughter of holiest gladness."

"I wonder how many Christians there are who so thoroughly believe God made them that they can laugh in God's name," MacDonald muses, "who understand that God invented laughter and gave it to His children. . . . The Lord of gladness delights in the laughter of a merry heart."

But true laughter, holy gladness, requires freedom—from the weight of the world's cares, from self-concern, from suspicion and envy, from regret and worry. It is the laughter of a child wholly at home in the arms of someone who loves her. And this, for MacDonald, is what it means when Jesus says we must become like little children: to trust that our King, the one toward whom all our prayers are bent, bends down to kiss us with the tender love of a perfect Father. We are free to laugh in his presence because we have nothing left to fear.

Jesus, the Child in the manger, came to gather the children—the young ones and the old ones growing young again—and to lead us to the One whose arms are spread open wide, welcoming us with joy.

Father in heaven, have mercy upon your child who comes before you weighed down by fear and sorrow. Break the chains of doubt that keep my heart from being free in your presence, and help me to trust that I am completely and eternally embraced by your love.
Teach me to laugh again. Amen.

Jennifer Trafton is the author of two novels for children, *The Rise and Fall of Mount Majestic* and *Henry and the Chalk Dragon*. She is a former managing editor of *Christian History* magazine.

Work out your salvation with fear and trembling, for it is God who works in you to will and to act in order to fulfill his good purpose.

(Philippians 2:12–13, NIV)

Sunrise hike at Lake Moraine

> *"I wish it need not have happened in my time," said Frodo. "So do I," said Gandalf, "and so do all who live to see such times. But that is not for them to decide. All we have to decide is what to do with the time that is given us."*
>
> — J. R. R. Tolkien, *The Lord of the Rings*

When I feel overwhelmed by the state of the world, or the problems I am facing; when all seems hopeless, and I don't know what to do, I am often reminded of this, my favorite scene in *The Lord of the Rings*. Here Gandalf gives Frodo a very precious gift—he limits Frodo's responsibility to the few things he can actually do something about. Dorothy Sayers echoes a similar idea in *The Nine Tailors*:

> It does not do for us to take too much thought for the morrow. It is better to follow the truth and leave the result in the hand of God. He can foresee where we cannot, because He knows all the facts.

In my more honest moments, I see how I can use the enormity of the situation, or my regret over past failures, or my worry about what might happen tomorrow to avoid doing the things that are actually within my power to do here and now. But a peace comes from resting within our limits as created beings, content to play the small role we have in the story God is weaving. Yet it is an active peace—we must actually get up, walk out the door, and do the thing we can do. The poor shepherds who witnessed the first Christmas Eve no doubt had many struggles and perhaps felt powerless and small in a large world, but there was something they could do: "Let's go to Bethlehem and see this thing that has happened..." And God used this simple effort for his glory.

Philippians 2:12–13 reminds me both that God is in sovereign control and that I must work; I must decide how to use the time he has given me. Like the shepherds I fear and tremble because God is at work. But this fear and trembling empowers me to do that thing I can do, overcoming that other fear and trembling—the one that comes from the brokenness of the world.

Dear Jesus, help me to focus on the one thing I can do today and to entrust to you how things will work out. Amen.

Langdon Palmer is pastor of Leverington Presbyterian Church in Philadelphia. His sermon podcasts related to the Inklings' works can be found at www.levpres.org.

*Therefore the Lord himself shall give you a sign;
behold, a virgin shall conceive, and bear a son,
and shall call his name Immanuel.*
(Isaiah 7:14, KJV)

The crocus heralds the coming spring.

> *The Christian story is precisely the story of one grand miracle . . . what is uncreated, eternal, came into nature, into human nature, descended into His own universe, and rose again, bringing nature up with Him.*
>
> —C. S. Lewis, *Miracles*

For the two decades between 1943 and his death in 1963, C. S. Lewis annually read his friend Dorothy L. Sayers's radio plays on the life of the Incarnate Christ, *The Man Born to Be King*. And every time, as he testified at Sayers's funeral in 1958, he was "deeply moved." Throughout Lewis's writings we see this emotional and imaginative engagement with the Incarnation—not just as a brief episode portrayed once a year in church pageants, but as the single central event that changes everything.

In his book *Miracles*, Lewis imagines Christ as a deep-sea diver working on a salvage project: plunging down into his own fallen creation "in order to bring the whole ruined world up with him to new life." In *The Lion, the Witch and the Wardrobe*, when the lion Aslan reenters the world he created, he breaks the hold of a long, hopeless winter, returning it to the new life of spring and restoring flesh and blood to hapless souls imprisoned as stone statues.

His sci-fi story *Perelandra* culminates in a hymn to God's "Great Dance": "In the Fallen World He prepared for Himself a body and was united with the Dust and made it glorious for ever. This is the end and final cause of all creating. . . . Blessed be He!"

How can we even imagine what this means for us, that we dust-creatures will be glorified and "brought up with him"? In *Mere Christianity* Lewis concludes: "The whole offer which Christianity makes is this: that we can, if we let God have his way, come to share in the life of Christ."

No wonder Lewis was so deeply moved by the Incarnation. So should we be too!

Lord, you have come to draw us up to you along with all of nature, to share with us your very life! This Advent, move us to wonder at your coming to earth as one of us—and to rejoice and be deeply moved at what it all means. Amen

Chris R. Armstrong serves as senior editor of *Christian History* magazine and as a program fellow at the Kern Family Foundation. He blogs at gratefultothedead.com and recently authored *Medieval Wisdom for Modern Christians*.

I am the living bread that came down from heaven.
Whoever eats this bread will live forever. This bread is my
flesh, which I will give for the life of the world.

(John 6:51, NIV)

Fire

*In final participation—since the death and resurrection—
the heart is fired from within by the Christ,
and it is for the heart to enliven the images.*

—Owen Barfield, *Saving the Appearances*

When I was a young Christian, I was told that there were "spiritual" things and there were "worldly" physical things, and what was physical should be set aside in favor of what was spiritual. Maybe you were told that too.

In his book *Saving the Appearances*, Owen Barfield—friend of C. S. Lewis, lawyer, and philosopher—tells me that I was wrong. Barfield is sometimes unorthodox, but on this particular point he is in line with Christian tradition: all of human history, stretching back into the depths of unrecorded time, is centered on the Incarnation. In this act the divine Logos that exists eternally beyond the physical world entered into it in the person of Jesus.

Only through the Incarnation, Barfield believed, could humans move from "original" to "final" participation. In original participation, which he identified with pre-Christian paganism, human beings experienced the divine presence as something outside themselves in the physical world. In the Old Testament, the ancient Hebrews rejected this concept and recognized God as a being wholly other than the physical world. But in the Incarnation, God entered not only into the physical world but into the human race in particular, so that through the Holy Spirit, people could consciously participate in the divine.

Because of this we are called to bring life to all creation; the physical world is no longer a purely material collection of "idols." The great spiritual struggle of our times, according to Barfield, is against a worldview in which physical things are nothing more than physical and no transcendent meaning exists. But the answer is not to go back to a paganism in which humans are the playthings of spiritual forces, but to go forward to a redeemed creation in which the light of the divine Logos shines through human minds and hearts into the world of nature and the artifacts of human ingenuity.

And this night, with this tiny baby in a manger, is the moment when everything changes.

*Lord, help us in the power of your Spirit to go forward
into your redeemed creation, fired by your love. Amen.*

Edwin Woodruff Tait is contributing editor at *Christian History*.

Jesus then said to them, "Truly, truly I say to you, it was not Moses who gave you the bread from heaven; my father gives you the true bread from heaven. For the bread of God is that which comes down from heaven, and gives life to the world."
(John 6:32–33, NRSV)

The Eucharist

It is not what God can give us, but God that we want.

—George MacDonald, *Wilfred Cumbermede*

George MacDonald was a seasoned old soul; what was true for him may have been more of an ideal for other pilgrims on the journey. The rest of us may feel more inclined to pray, "Father, forgive us, for we know not what we want."

We seek a gilded afterlife when we could have Eternal Life. We seek breadcrumbs of earthly pleasure when we could join a heavenly banquet. We avoid pain when we could embrace joy. We plead for words of comfort and light, but our darkness does not comprehend the Word.

Help us, Lord. We ask for a roadmap to heaven when the Way, the Truth, the Life stands right before us. We want the crown without the cross, and we fix our gaze on the crown more than on the King. We look to Glory, but others do not see the glory when they look at us.

We do not ask too much in prayer, but too little. We follow the one who multiplied the loaves and do not see the bread of life. We want to quench the thirst of this moment, but do not ask for living water, the cup of heaven.

The Everlasting took human form so that we might lift our eyes from the gifts to the Giver. He emptied himself so that from his fullness we might receive grace upon grace. The baby lay in a feeding trough so we might not be forever hungry. The child spoke in his Father's house, so we might put away childish things. The man told us that we must die to live, that sorrow would turn to joy, that those who seek will find. He rose that we might rise. He came to be with us for a time so that we might be with him forever.

*Lord, teach us to know what we want,
to want what you want, to want you. Amen.*

David C. Downing is codirector, with his wife Crystal, of the Marion E. Wade Center at Wheaton College, Illinois. He is the author of numerous works, including *The Most Reluctant Convert* and *Planets in Peril*, both on C. S. Lewis.

But the angel said to them, "Do not be afraid;
for see—I am bringing you good news of great joy for all
the people: to you is born this day in the city of David
a Savior, who is the Messiah, the Lord.
(Luke 2:10–11, NRSV)

Michigan's Pictured Rocks National Lakeshore

The Scotch catechism says that man's chief end is "to glorify God and enjoy Him forever." But we shall then know that these are the same thing. Fully to enjoy is to glorify.

—C. S. Lewis, *Reflections on the Psalms*

When I was a child, reared on what Lewis calls the "Scotch catechism" (the *Westminster Shorter Catechism*), I never quite grasped what its first answer meant when it said we are to "enjoy" God forever. As an adult, partly from studying Jonathan Edwards, I came to see that the joy is the delight of encountering "the beauty of the Lord."

Beauty is a central motif in much of Christian thought, as it is in Lewis's. When he speaks of our deepest longings, it is always longing for that beauty. And the joy that surprises us is that of actually finding what we long for in the depths of our being.

Beauty has a sort of magnetic power that draws us to it. If we encounter great beauty in nature, in art, or in a great work of music, we want to keep telling others about it. But nothing compares to the beauty of love, and the highest beauty is the beauty of the most perfect love. It is the astonishing love of the perfect being for the utterly undeserving, as seen in Christ's death for us on the cross. Lewis explains our need to praise God for such love as being like that of lovers who cannot stop talking about their love.

That helps explain a Christian paradox. In effecting our salvation, God does everything, yet he waits for our own free action. If we have eyes to see and ears to hear the "good news of great joy," we will be captivated by the beauty of Christ's sacrificial love. Yet none of our actions are more truly free than our overwhelming response of love and joy.

Father, help us to be renewed today and each day by the sheer joy of experiencing your love in Christ. Amen.

George Marsden is a historian and the author of *C. S. Lewis's Mere Christianity: A Biography*. He has also written on Jonathan Edwards and on the history of American evangelicalism.

Suddenly an angel of the Lord stood by their side, the splendor of the Lord blazed around them, and they were terror-stricken. But the angel said to them, "Do not be afraid!"... And in a flash there appeared with the angel a vast host of the armies of Heaven, praising God, saying, "Glory to God in the highest Heaven!"

(Luke 2: 9–10, 13–14 J. B. Phillips New Testament)

Young stars in a nebula in the Small Magellanic Cloud

The famous saying "God is love," it is generally assumed, means that God is like our immediate emotional indulgence, not that the meaning of love ought to have something of the "otherness" and terror of God.

—Charles Williams, *He Came Down from Heaven*

In these few words, Charles Williams eloquently captures the paradox of the Incarnation. God is love: we see this powerfully embodied in the way he chose to come to us—in the incarnate form of a tiny, vulnerable baby. Indeed he is Emmanuel, "God-with-us"—not remote or far away, but here and now, come to us in the humble surroundings of a lowly stable, not in a palace or on a throne.

At the same time, the glorious "other," of which Williams writes, is also present. It can be seen when "the splendor of the Lord blazed around [the shepherds] and they were terror-stricken" and in the angelic host filling the night sky, proclaiming "Glory to God in the highest."

Throughout Scripture encounters with the transcendent are so striking, so frightening, that those involved are inevitably told: "Do not be afraid." Even Moses, for all of his intimacy with God, was still unable to see the face of God in the fullness of his glory, and live.

In his seven novels, Charles Williams often depicts the great fear that arose when his fictional characters encountered the transcendent. As an Anglican he was well-versed in a liturgy that acknowledges the loving accessibility of God as well as his holiness. Thus Williams would have embraced the necessity of incorporating both elements in our worship and knowledge of God: the tiny incarnate baby and the overwhelming glory.

Because God is love, "he came down from heaven: by the power of the Holy Spirit, he became incarnate from the Virgin Mary and was made man," as the creeds say. And only through the loving, atoning work of Christ, the incarnate one, can we, as sinful, finite beings, approach the throne of the Most High, the glorious, righteous Holy One.

Thanks be to God.

Enable us to bring your love, Lord, into the ordinary everyday reality of our lives so that others might begin to see your transcendent Glory shining forth even in this dark, broken world. Amen.

Marjorie Lamp Mead is associate director of Marion E. Wade Center at Wheaton College, Illinois, where much of her work has focused on Sayers and Lewis.

The Son is the image of the invisible God, the one who is first over all creation, because all things were created by him…. He existed before all things, and all things are held together in him. (Colossians 1:15–17, CEB)

No plastic children

> *"He came down from Heaven" can almost be transposed into "Heaven drew earth up into it," and locality, limitation, sleep, sweat, footsore weariness, frustration, pain, doubt, and death, are, from before all worlds, known by God from within.*
>
> —C. S. Lewis, *Letters to Malcolm: Chiefly on Prayer*

It's easy to imagine Jesus as the plastic baby in the nativity scene on our mantel. He "sleeps in heavenly peace" while "no crying he makes," after all.

Yet as I cuddle my wiggling daughter, as she babbles or tries to lick the cookie crumbs off my fingers, as I look into her eyes and stroke back hair from a face that I would whisk away to Egypt in a heartbeat, I see the living, breathing Jesus; the Jesus who learned to walk and delighted his mom and dad with each new word; the Jesus who enjoyed good food and worked with his hands; the Jesus who stood up to bullies and cried with his friends.

In coming down from heaven, Jesus was God's "yes" to both the joy and pain of human existence. He allowed himself to be human through and through: hunger, fatigue, blisters, and all. He felt deeply—frustration, anger, betrayal, and grief, but also affection, humor, amazement, and love.

The same Word of God that made humans in God's own image and then declared, "This is very good!" became flesh and blood and lived among us. In becoming human God proclaimed a blessing on the complicated realities of life. There is no joy without struggle, no love without loss, no connection without the possibility of brokenness. And God himself, the Word who created our world for the messiness of relationship, by stepping into this uncertainty and possibility, declared, "This is very good!"

I imagine that the Jesus in the nativity set on my mantel cries when he's hungry. That's what my babies do; honestly, sometimes I do too. He also smiles and coos when his tummy is full and finds comfort in the arms of his mama. This is the complicated reality of being human; we need each other. It's a reflection of who God made us to be because it's a reflection of who God is: community.

In Jesus God entered the community of creation so that creation could enter the community of God.

> *Dear Jesus, as I experience the joy and pain of being human today, remind me that you've been there and can help me hold it all together. Amen.*

Emily Ralph Servant is a leadership minister for Franconia Mennonite Conference and an adjunct professor of mission and theology at Eastern Mennonite Seminary.

*When they saw that the star had stopped, they were
overwhelmed with joy. On entering the house, they saw the
child with Mary his mother; and they knelt down
and paid him homage.*

(Matthew 2:10–11, NRSV)

The morning star

Far above ... the night-sky was still dim and pale. There, peeping among the cloud-wrack above a dark tor high up in the mountains, Sam saw a white star twinkle for a while. The beauty of it smote his heart, as he looked up out of the forsaken land, and hope returned to him. For like a shaft, clear and cold, the thought pierced him that in the end the Shadow was only a small and passing thing: there was light and high beauty forever beyond its reach.

—J. R. R.Tolkien, *The Lord of the Rings*

We might not know exactly what the star looked like that led the Magi to Jesus 2,000 years ago. Was it a comet, perhaps a large one that drew the attention of many? Or maybe one so faint that only those who studied the night sky carefully even noticed it?

Even if we haven't seen a comet, most of us have experienced the beauty of the night sky. We have also seen the morning star. Like the promise of the coming Messiah sung by angels to shepherds, the morning star heralds the approaching dawn. With that clear, cold, beautiful shaft of light, it sings: Morning is coming! The sun will rise soon!

Yet for all its beauty, it still comes after a long night. In the midst of deepest darkness, our eyes, drawn to the heavens, catch the glimpse of hope the morning star heralds—like Sam catching a glimpse of the star Eärendil even from the shadows of Mordor. So too did the Magi's star appear over Bethlehem in the darkest of times. Israel languished in captivity, released from 70 years of slavery in Babylon only to fall into a much longer oppression by Rome. When would the longed-for Messiah come? When would the promised freedom appear? When could the people sing: *Morning has come!*?

The answer to that question came to shepherds watching their flock by night. In the midst of a seemingly hopeless situation, a sign of hope: A baby born in a manger. Good news. The sun has risen! Christmas Day is here!

So too, even in midst of the darkness of our age—the pain, sin, and sorrow that plague this world—we are reminded of hope. However dark our darkness feels, the shadow that breeds that darkness is just a vain and passing thing. The hope we greet on Christmas morning is the lasting reality.

Lord Jesus, let the hope of your promises and the beauty of the Christmas gospel smite our hearts even in the midst of whatever darkness surrounds us. Amen.

Matthew Dickerson, a professor at Middlebury College, is the author of the Daegmon War fantasy series, narrative nonfiction *The Voices of Rivers*, and several books and essays about J. R. R. Tolkien and C. S. Lewis.

The people walking in darkness have seen a great light;
on those living in the land of deep darkness
a light has dawned.

(Isaiah 9:2, NIV)

Christmas crib figures

Among the asses (stubborn I as they)
I see my Saviour where I looked for hay.

—C. S. Lewis, "The Nativity," from
The Collected Poems of C. S. Lewis: A Critical Edition

Asses and hay. Seeing and looking. At first glance these things seem to have little in common and still less to do with Advent. But, as usually happens when it comes to the Good News, looking more deeply lets us see more clearly. And so too with Lewis, who in his little Advent poem "The Nativity," helps us as he so often does to move past merely looking to truly see.

Both in the *Chronicles of Narnia* and in Lewis's letters of that period, an ass almost always describes someone or something present but missing the point. "What you see and what you hear depends a great deal on where you are standing. It also depends on what sort of person you are," Lewis suggests. This reminds me of the dwarfs in *The Last Battle* who would not be taken in; who,

when they enter the stable and are presented with a great feast in the glorious light of Aslan's Country, can see only hay, filth, and darkness.

Their problem comes from the distinction between looking and seeing. We too often look only for hay (and wood, and stubble), when at a second glance we might instead see our Savior. For we, too, walk in a land of deep darkness, and so often we miss the things rushing by us that might let us see Christ, disguised as everything. Lewis reminds us that if we will really see instead of simply look, we might catch a glimpse of the Light of the World, dawning upon us all in this season of Advent. So let us stand in that stable and look for the Savior. And let us become the sort of people who might truly see him.

O, Lord, give us eyes to see, and help us, especially in this season,
to find you everywhere, breaking through the darkness
and bringing us to your feast. Amen.

Andrew Lazo is a C. S. Lewis scholar and delightedly married to author and fellow contributor Christin Ditchfield.

*We declare to you what was from the beginning,
what we have heard, what we have seen with our eyes,
what we have looked at and touched with our hands,
concerning the word of life.*

(Luke 2:34–35, NRSV)

Christ Church Cathedral, Oxford, where Sayers was baptized

You are quite right in thinking that for Christians the emphasis is not primarily on the teaching but on the Person of Christ. That does not mean that the teaching is unimportant, but it is important because He is Who He is, and not the other way round.

—Dorothy L. Sayers, letter to Maurice Browne, November 22, 1946

Dorothy L. Sayers wrote the above words to an appreciative reader who asked her a question about the Christian faith. Her correspondents were usually ordinary laypeople who gave no possible advantage to promoting Sayers's career or burnishing her reputation among the elite. She claimed, in a letter to C. S. Lewis, that "all spiritual experience is a closed book to me. . . . All the apparatus I have by which to apprehend anything at all is intellect and imagination."

Maybe so. Yet in so often explaining the basic dogmas of Christianity—patiently, charitably, accessibly, and with no reference to herself—she nudged any number of correspondents toward Christian belief and, therefore, the possibility of enjoying thought, creativity, and even experience in fellowship with God.

For myself, after a lifetime studying obviously authentic, but also extraordinarily diverse, expressions of Christian faith in the past—and witnessing in my own life a fairly wide diversity of faith expressions as well—Sayers's advice to focus on the person of Christ makes absolute sense. Further sentences from this same letter explain why some who believe will do so primarily with the heart, others with the soul, and still others with the mind: "The doctrine of human personality depends upon the personality of God. God is . . . the same Person that was manifested as a man in Christ, and He has made us persons in His own image. Our business in this mortal life is to build up the potential personality in us (by the grace and power available through the life of Christ) into the true personality God wants us to have. . . . God wants us to be real persons, he wants us to be ourselves."

Whether your faith is centered on heart, mind, or soul, God in Christ welcomes all that you are.

Lord, I come to you as myself, bringing my heart, my mind, and my soul to the altar. Take what I have and use it for your glory. Amen.

Mark A. Noll is the author of *A History of Christianity in the United States and Canada* and professor emeritus at both Wheaton College and Notre Dame.

And she gave birth to her firstborn son and wrapped him in bands of cloth, and laid him in a manger, because there was no place for them in the inn.

(Luke 2:7, NRSV)

Nativity scene

In our world too, a stable once had something inside it that was bigger than our whole world.

—C. S. Lewis, *The Last Battle*

Most people enjoy solving a mystery. In today's world a mystery usually involves either figuring out who did a crime or who's responsible for someone's death (and sometimes both). As human beings we naturally want an explanation about what happened and how it was done. However the greatest mystery of all involves a miracle beyond our ability to understand.

Accepting the fact of Jesus's birth into our earthly realm involves believing notions outside of our comprehension. How could something "bigger than our whole world," as Queen Lucy rightly states in C. S. Lewis's fictional Narnia, fit in a stable? And yet that's exactly what happened!

Jesus, who is God, took upon himself our human nature to live among us. He accomplished this by becoming the firstborn son of his earthly parents, Mary and Joseph. So the most powerful force in the universe entered his own creation at the weakest point in a human being's life. The baby Jesus depended upon earthly parents, and yet, as God, he did not need to rely on anybody. We are unable to process ideas like these because they are contradictory to our finite minds.

Thus, by faith, we accept a truth beyond our ability to understand. This miraculous birth demonstrates that God has such love and compassion for us that he sent his Son, Jesus, into our world, though he is actually so much bigger than the manger he was born in. Only by embracing this mysterious miracle that we can't figure out can its truth impact our life.

Father, help me to let truths that I cannot understand speak into my life and make a difference in me. May the miracle of your birth always amaze me, even as it remains a mystery. Amen.

William O'Flaherty is the author of *The Misquotable C. S. Lewis* and an enhanced study guide to *The Screwtape Letters* entitled *C. S. Lewis Goes to Hell.*

*Then Simeon blessed them and said to [Jesus's] mother Mary,
"This child is destined for the falling and the rising of many
in Israel, and to be a sign that will be opposed so that the
inner thoughts of many will be revealed—and a sword will
pierce your own soul too.*

(Luke 2:34–35, NRSV)

Simeon blesses the child Jesus in the temple.

All things are possible with God,
but all things are not easy.

—George MacDonald, *Unspoken Sermons*, 2nd series, "Life"

"Christmas is coming!" the secular world says—time to put up the decorations, plan the parties, buy and wrap the gifts. "Christmas is coming!" the church says—time to hold the pageants and sing the joyful songs.

Yet for many at this season, both the world's cheer and the church's eager excitement are difficult. The days speak to us of past sorrows such as the death of loved ones, or of future fears about family and jobs and the state of this tumultuous world.

It's easy to think of the beautiful moment captured in many nativity scenes—adoring mother, peaceful child—and forget that Mary had to cope not only with all the usual troubles of child raising but with danger, displacement, and even prophecies that reminded her that her adorable baby boy would end up as a sign of political and spiritual turmoil. She probably knew that the last line of Simeon's prophecy meant she would outlive her son.

George MacDonald's art, too, was born from suffering. He struggled with health problems from childhood, fought with his congregation, and for much of his life was short of money. He knew the same soul-piercing sword as the Virgin Mary, outliving four of his children and one granddaughter.

Today we remember that we serve a Christ who came as Mary's helpless baby so that he could understand our suffering. With *that* Christ all things are possible, and he walks with us.

Dear Jesus, thank you for being with me always,
even when things are not easy. I commit my sorrows into your
hand as I await your coming. Amen.

Jennifer Woodruff Tait is managing editor of *Christian History* magazine and an Episcopal priest. She lives in Berea, Kentucky.

And having been warned in a dream not to return to Herod, they left for their own country by another road.

(Matthew 2:12, NRSV)

Addison's Walk, Magdalen College, Oxford

Herod had his place, therefore, in the miracle play of Bethlehem, because he is the menace to the Church Militant, and shows it from the first as under persecution and fighting for its life. For those who think this a discord, it is a discord that sounds simultaneously with the Christmas bells.

—G. K. Chesterton, *The Everlasting Man*

On this side of heaven, Christmas comes tied up with green ribbon and red tape. The Magi's rerouting, along with the Holy Family's, reminds us that Christmas is a time for celebrating light, but that such light shines in the darkness. Chesterton's words recall how the Magi's own gifts at the birth represented kingship, deity, and death. How can a holy nativity be bound so closely to a horrific mass infanticide? Or a homecoming census entwined with such desperate exile?

Our lives reflect these same paradoxes today, and so the nativity story remains as relevant as ever in its refrain of how God's guidance helps those in danger and despair navigate the politics of pain.

Dreams drive the action in the nativity story. Those Christmas angels were busy! Through dreams Christmas leads us from the Old Testament into the New. The transformation of the spirit helps us navigate the twists and turns of the world.

Pilgrimages obedient to our dreams illustrate just how Emmanuel is indeed God fully with us, including in the most secret places of ourselves, even when we think he cannot be, even when we cannot think at all.

Once transformed by Christ, we must take a new path to "return" to our lives. Birth requires death, and death leads to birth, as T. S. Eliot's famous poem, "The Journey of the Magi," reminds us. If it is a discord, it is a discord that sounds simultaneously with the Christmas bells, indeed. For the journey is ours as much as it is for those awaiting our arrival, and the transformation of all of us rings far beyond our wildest dreams.

Dear Lord, in our broken world there often seems to be more strife than joy. Help us find among the notes of discord a new song. When all hope seems lost, and we ourselves lost with it, show us another way back to you. Amen.

Carolyn Weber completed her doctorate in Romantic literature at Oxford University. She is currently an author, speaker, and professor at Heritage College & Seminary and Western University in London, Canada.

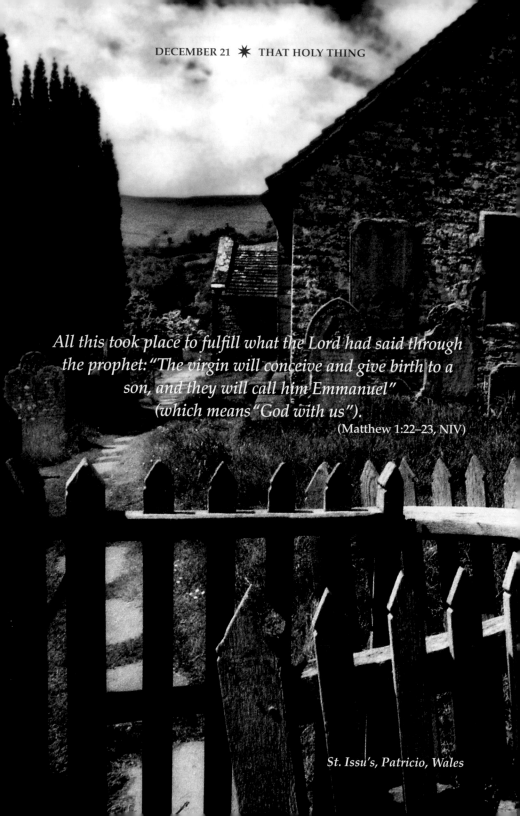

All this took place to fulfill what the Lord had said through the prophet: "The virgin will conceive and give birth to a son, and they will call him Emmanuel" (which means "God with us").

(Matthew 1:22–23, NIV)

St. Issu's, Patricio, Wales

They all were looking for a king
to slay their foes and lift them high;
Thou cam'st, a little baby thing
That made a woman cry.

—George MacDonald, hymn, "That Holy Thing"

*T*he bone-chilling sea-damp is what I remember most from our first Christmas Eve service in Scotland. That, and the singing.

Romantic on paper: a fishing village, an ancient stone church, the bells . . . but reality included huddling together for warmth. As we shivered the congregation rose for a hymn new only to us: "That Holy Thing."

"That Holy Thing" is not a typical Christmas carol; MacDonald reminds us that holy is not comfortable, let alone predictable. We want holiness to sweep away all ills and be cozy and Christmasy too. But holy does not avoid pain or difficulty, even while making way for good. It facilitates vulnerability; It usurps assumptions; it invites—sometimes even causes—tears.

The Child comes and instead sweeps away our ideas of triumph. A "little baby thing," the long-awaited Messiah is born into a low-income, scandal-threatened, displaced family. This seed of royal lineage is destined to become a border-crossing refugee before he is old enough for school. Instead of conquering the opposition and asserting the rights of his people, he arrives as a helpless infant that makes a woman cry.

Here is real flesh-and-blood, breaking forth via real sweat-and-tears, into this real dust-and-mud world of his own Triune making. Woven into the pain of his unglamorous arrival is the promise of goodness beyond conception, but not in the way that even those who expect challenges expect. Christ asks not for political strength or financial security or even familial ease. Rather he asks that we welcome weakness, embrace the uncomfortable, step into that which may hurt—and promises that throughout he will be with us.

The invitation is into an unpredictable holiness that is sometimes joyful and sometimes hard. But Emmanuel's chosen identity pledges also, always, this: that even when huddled against cold or tears, we are never, ever, alone.

Emmanuel, make us ever more aware of your abiding loving presence; may that give us courage this Christmas to be humble servants of your love in spaces we might otherwise avoid. Amen.

Kirstin Jeffrey Johnson is a writer, George MacDonald scholar, and director of the Linlathen Lectures. She lives in the Ottawa Valley, Canada.

ST ISSU'S, PATRICIO, WALES—PHOTO BY BRUCE S. JEFFREY

Wait for the Lord; be strong and take heart
and wait for the Lord.

(Psalm 27:14, NIV)

Gifts to be opened Christmas Day

It is the very essence of a festival that it breaks upon one brilliantly and abruptly. . . . it is essential that there should be a clear black line between it and the time going before. And all the old wholesome customs in connection with Christmas were to the effect that one should not touch or see or know or speak of something before the actual coming of Christmas Day.

—G. K. Chesterton, *Illustrated London News*, January 12, 1907

T he liturgical color for Advent is the same as for Lent. Purple is not the Christian symbol of royalty but of what Martin Luther called the heart bruised beneath the millstone. "The human heart is like a millstone in a mill," said Luther; "when you put wheat under it, it turns and grinds and bruises the wheat to flour; if you put no wheat, it still grinds on, but then 'tis itself it grinds and wears away." Advent calls us to let God pulverize the poor wheat of our sinful and errant lives, turning it into the flour that becomes nourishing bread for others. Without a penitent Advent, Christmas is an empty jollity, a grinding of ourselves back into dust, into nothing.

Chesterton's insistence on the "clear black line" also keeps time itself from becoming homogeneous, a mere succession of one thing after another, with no moment or event to be set apart and honored for its own unique significance. Our refusal to make such clear temporal demarcations is everywhere evident. All Hallows' Eve bleeds back into September, Christmas begins even before Thanksgiving has arrived, and Advent is lost altogether.

We will not wait upon the Lord. We want everything, even holy things, to happen now and not later. Living by *chronos* (clock time) rather than *kairos* (holy time), even Christians become a hurried and harried and impatient people. The Christian year teaches us how to mark clear lines, how to wait, and thus how to celebrate. Its sharply drawn seasons serve to renarrate the entire Christian story. It enables us to live according to God's own calendar: from Advent to Christmas, on to Epiphany and Lent, finally to Easter and Pentecost. Let all heaven and earth rejoice, therefore, when we cross the clear black line at midnight on Christmas Eve and not a minute before!

Help us to wait patiently and penitently for your coming, O Lord, so that we might be transformed into humble loaves of bread whose wheat and leaven come from you, the Bread of Life. Amen.

Ralph Wood teaches Christian theology in relation to literary texts at Baylor University in Waco, Texas.

*Blessed (praised, glorified) be the Lord,
the God of Israel, because He has visited us and
brought redemption to His people, and He has raised
up a horn of salvation [a mighty and valiant Savior]
for us in the house of David His servant—
just as He promised.*
(Luke 1:68–70, AMP)

Christmas horns

> *"And when you put this horn to your lips and blow it, then, wherever you are, I think help of some kind will come to you."*
>
> —C. S. Lewis, Father Christmas to Susan in
> *The Lion, the Witch and the Wardrobe*

*I*t was a Christmas I'd never forget—my last Christmas as a single woman, my last Christmas surrounded by all my family and friends in a community in which I'd lived for over 30 years. I could hardly believe that in less than two weeks, I'd be getting married—a dream come true, the long-awaited answer to countless prayers—and moving halfway across the country to start a new life at midlife. The thought both thrilled and terrified me.

On Christmas morning I gazed around the crowded living room at my parents, my four siblings, and their spouses and children. Emotions ran high, each of us trying to savor and treasure every last moment together.

When it was my turn, I opened a gift from my brother David: a replica of Queen Susan's horn from the *Chronicles of Narnia*. With it came a note reminding me that my family would always be there for me, even when far away, and that if I was ever in any trouble or distress, I needed only to call, and "help of some kind" would come to me.

What a precious gift!

Sometimes we all feel anxious. There are moments we all feel forgotten or abandoned, lost in our sin and sorrow and suffering. But just as Susan had the promise of her horn, we have the promise of God's horn of salvation—Jesus. Christmas reminds us that because of him, we have hope, we have help, we have comfort and strength. The Scriptures tell us that all who call on him will be saved (Rom 10:13). Jesus will always come to rescue us and "enable us to serve him without fear in holiness and righteousness before him all of our days" (Luke 1:75 NIV).

Hallelujah!

> *Thank you, Father, for keeping your promise. Thank you for sending Jesus to my rescue. Remind me to call on him constantly, and fill my heart this season with the joy of your salvation! Amen.*

Christin Ditchfield is the author of the best-selling *A Family Guide to Narnia: Biblical Truths in C. S. Lewis's the Chronicles of Narnia*. She is married to Lewis scholar Andrew Lazo.

Have this mind among yourselves, which is yours in Christ Jesus, who, though he was in the form of God, did not count equality with God a thing to be grasped, but emptied himself, taking the form of a servant, being born in the likeness of men.
(Philippians 2: 5–7, RSV)

Children's Christmas pageant

> *The Christian faith is the most exciting drama that ever staggered the imagination of man—and the dogma is the drama.*
>
> —Dorothy L. Sayers, "The Greatest Drama Ever Staged"

Christmas provided my first experience of drama as I joined children in bathrobes playing Magi, while others, topped with pillow cases, portrayed shepherds at the manger. Only later did I learn the historical significance of such performances. Christians as early as the tenth century formally acted out the Advent story. Medieval priests recognized that Christian belief is inherently exciting or, as Sayers put it, "the dogma is the drama."

Hence, when I taught Medieval Drama at a famous secular university, I required students to read the Bible stories upon which medieval plays were based so that we could discuss interpretive choices made by the dramatists. Very careful to not impose my Christian beliefs, I never once preached the gospel or shared my testimony; I merely exposed students to the medieval texts and the Biblical material that inspired them. At the end of the course, numerous students expressed amazement about how much more sophisticated Christianity was than they had been led to believe. One, an unwed mother, shared with me, "After studying medieval drama I can believe that Jesus still loves me."

But after reading effusive student evaluations praising my course, university officials pulled Medieval Drama from my schedule, never allowing me to teach the course again. Like Herod suspicious of the Magi, those in charge often revile the search for a lord other than the ones they approve of. Jesus, in contrast, gave up all power, as the Magi explain to Herod in an eleventh-century play: "He whom in his own special vastness / The heavens, the earth and the wide seas cannot contain, / Born from virgin womb, is laid in a manger."

The dogma is indeed the drama.

> *Dear God, you have called us to continue dramatizing dogma by following the example of Christ. Thank you for the script of the Bible to direct us as we live out our roles as children of God. Amen.*

Crystal Downing is codirector, with her husband, David, of the Marion E. Wade Center at Wheaton College, Illinois. Her first book, *Writing Performances: The Stages of Dorothy L. Sayers*, inspired three more books about the relationship between faith and culture, the most recent being *Salvation from Cinema: The Medium Is the Message*.

When you search for me, you will find me;
if you seek me with all your heart.

(Jeremiah 29:13, NRSV)

The Adoration of the Magi

Continue seeking Him with seriousness.
Unless He wanted you, you would not be wanting Him.

—C. S. Lewis, letter to Genia Goelz, June 13, 1951

𝔐any Christmas cards show three kings walking toward Bethlehem. Yet the Bible doesn't tell us that they were kings, nor that there were three of them! We're told that they were "wise men from the East" and that they carried three different gifts, but that's all. The important thing is that they came—not what their status was or how many of them there were.

In the church calendar, they arrive not on the 25th of December, but on the 6th of January, which is celebrated as "the feast of the manifestation of Christ to the Gentiles." As my birthday is January 6, I've always had particular interest in this part of the Bible story.

The Wise Men come "late,"—twelve days after the birth of the Savior—but they still come. They come from "outside"—as Gentiles, not members of the people of Israel—but they still come. They come a long way—but they still come.

They come to him because he came to them. He came first and foremost in the newborn baby lying in the manger. But he also came to the Wise Men by means of the star that announced his birth and by means of their intelligence and courage, which inspired them to undergo this grueling and hazardous journey.

For Jesus is not only the Truth and the Life, he is also the Way. As we go toward him, we are already meeting him every step of the way. Unless he wanted us, we would not be wanting him.

I once received a Christmas card that had no picture on it, but just the words: "Wise men still seek Him." May we be wise men, wise women, wise children this Christmas.

O God, who by the leading of a star revealed your Son Jesus Christ to the Wise Men: mercifully grant us wisdom to know that we would not be seeking him unless he was first seeking us. Amen.

Michael Ward, the author of *Planet Narnia*, is a Fellow of Blackfriars Hall, University of Oxford, and professor of apologetics at Houston Baptist University.

Marion E. Wade Center

"A living literary center of scholarly, artistic, and ongoing spiritual renewal"

The Marion E. Wade Center at Wheaton College offers a collection of resources available nowhere else in the world. The transformative thought and writings of these seven British Christian authors provide a distinctive blend of *intellect, imagination,* and *faith.*

Visit the Wade Center museum and see exhibits and display items such as Lewis's family wardrobe, Tolkien's writing desk, artwork related to our authors, and much more. Read for fun—as well as to discover the excitement of unpublished sources—in the Kilby Reading Room.

Visit the Wade Center, and peek into the Lewis family wardrobe!

WADE CENTER AUTHORS

C. S. Lewis
J. R. R. Tolkien
Dorothy L. Sayers
G. K. Chesterton
George MacDonald
Owen Barfield
Charles Williams

Enjoy our many programs, lectures, and events either in person or online through our YouTube channel and website. To learn more about the Wade Center's programs and publications, visit us online at *wheaton.edu/wade*.

Hours: Mon-Fri, 9am-4pm; Sat 9am-noon
Contact: 630.752.5908; wade@wheaton.edu
Address: 351 E. Lincoln Ave., Wheaton, Illinois

/thewadecenter /thewadecenter /WadeCenter Wade Center Podcast

Wade Center PODCAST

Listen to the Wade Center Podcast to enjoy conversations with scholars and figures related to the Wade's seven authors. Hear discussions with Douglas Gresham, Patti Callahan Henry, Malcolm Guite, Michael Ward, Philip Ryken and many more! Listen on iTunes, Spotify, YouTube or visit *wheaton.edu/listen*.

Know your story, embrace the journey.

UNCOVER YOUR FAITH HERITAGE ONE STORY AT A TIME.

Subscribe for FREE!

Mention source code ADV2019.

ChristianHistoryMagazine.org/subscribe • 1-800-468-0458

CHRISTIAN HISTORY
magazine